What I WORE Today

GINA LEE BEAN (UK)

MARLOES DE VRIES (THE NETHERLANDS)

JENNY McCLURE (UK)

LIZZY STEWART (UK)

MARI JAYE BEE (USA)

DIOGO MACHADO (BRAZIL)

NEIL SLORANCE (UK)

JO WANT (UK)

What I WORE Today

DOODLE YOURSELF INTO A STYLE ICON WITH...

Hello!

Gemma Correll

spruce

AN HACHETTE UK COMPANY

First published in Great Britain in 2011 by Spruce
a division of Octopus Publishing Group Ltd
Endeavour House, 189 Shaftesbury Avenue, London, WC2H 8JY
www.octopusbooks.co.uk

Text and Design © Octopus Publishing Group Ltd 2012
Illustrations © Gemma Correll

Distributed in the US by
Hachette Book Group USA
237 Park Avenue
New York, NY 10017, USA

Distributed in Canada by
Canadian Manda Group
165 Dufferin Street
Toronto, Ontario, Canada M6K 3H6

Gemma Correll asserts the moral right to be identified as the author of
this work

ISBN-13: 978-1-846-01395-9

A CIP catalogue record for this book is available from the British
Library

Printed and bound in China

10 9 8 7 6 5 4 3 2 1

NOTES

This book contains the opinions and ideas of the author. The author and
publisher disclaim all responsibility for any liability, loss or risk, personal
or otherwise, that is incurred as a consequence, directly or indirectly, of
the use and application of any of the contents of this book.

This is Mr. Norman Pickles.
He looks CONFUSED, perhaps
because he can't read ... (yet)

CONTENTS

Introduction

You don't have to be a fashionista to have fun doodling designs and outfits. Scribble, sketch, and doodle your way through a year's worth of your favorite outfits, accessories—and even your fashion mistakes.

What I Wore Today is a Flickr group and blog (and now a book, too!) created and curated by illustrator and proud owner of Mr. Norman Pickles the pug, Gemma Correll (that's me!). The idea came to me while I was browsing online, admiring the style of fashion-forward folks on street fashion blogs like The Sartorialist and user-curated sites such as LookBook, as well as the various blogs and groups where users can upload photos of themselves in their favorite stylish outfits. As an unphotogenic illustrator who spends a large proportion of her time wearing pajamas and other equally uninspiring outfits, I decided to draw what I wore instead.

YOUR
AUTHOR

The idea was pretty popular, so I decided to set up a group on image-hosting site Flickr where others could upload their own designs. The group soon gained thousands of members from all over the world. The artists range from professional designers to casual scribblers, male and female and from all age groups. The artworks are drawn, painted, collaged—there's even a hand-sewn 'What I Wore Today' doll! Some of the illustrations are annotated with notes about the artist's day—what they thought, felt, ate, drank, and saw that day, what the weather was like, or what music they listened to. There are drawings of outfits that have been worn to yoga classes, while doing the dishes, and even at the dentist! Being an individual is more important than following trends. Trends come and go, so experiment, learn what suits you, and what you're comfortable wearing. Dress for yourself, not for anyone else. Style and taste are subjective. Wear your clothes with a sense of humor and confidence. Clashing colors? Who cares? Last season's skirt length? So what? It doesn't matter what anybody else thinks. It's not all about buying your clothes from the trendiest stores or looking like celebs in magazines, either. The media bombards us with images of the 'perfect' bodies of celebrities—but remember, the photos have often been touched up and the celebs have good plastic surgeons!

Fashion isn't all about the clothes—let's not forget the accessories, the shoes, and the hairstyles. A simple outfit can be completely transformed by a statement* necklace or an eye-catching tote bag. Look for great accessories at craft fairs and on shopping sites such as Etsy.com—or just make your own.

Don't waste time trying to reach some unattainable goal. It's so much more important to be happy as you are.

Dressing well doesn't have to mean spending loads of money. Shopping on a budget doesn't mean buying cheaply made chain store clothes, either. Thrift shops are treasure troves for vintage items. Buying vintage clothes is eco-friendly too! Visiting yard sales, is great fun - you rarely go home with whatever it was that you originally set out to buy... but you'll often find something even better!

(fashion-talk for something really interesting, unique or pretty)

When buying cheap fashion, ask yourself, are you buying it because you really like it or because it's cheap? Visiting yard sales and flea markets, in your hometown and on vacation, is a lot of fun—you rarely go home with whatever it was you originally set out to buy... but you'll often find something even better! Don't go hunting for what's fashionable 'right now,' but look for interesting shapes and patterns, or classics that never go out of style (but hey, if you can rock those canary yellow hot pants all year round, go for it!*). Check the attic, or your parents' closets, for forgotten fashion gems. Who knows, mom's old '80s batwing sweater could be your new favorite item. Remember, when buying secondhand clothes, watch out for stains and moth holes and try things on wherever possible. Body shapes have changed over the decades and so has sizing, so a size 12 today is not the same as a size 12 from ten years ago—which would be a size 10 today.

Mix and match vintage and modern clothes for a fun, eclectic look.

This book is full of handy hints and tips for creating your very own one-of-a-kind items. Also check out websites like craftster.org and burdastyle.com for tips and patterns. It's worth getting a decent sewing machine, but that doesn't necessarily mean the most expensive one with the fanciest settings. A basic but sturdy one will be just fine. If you can't afford to buy one by yourself, why not club together with some friends and share one?

Some cities have open sewing workshops where, for a small fee, you can rent a sewing machine. You could set up a craft night locally with some friends and get together to sew, sketch, have a gossip, share tips, books and resources, and nibble some cupcakes.

You don't have to be an artist to use this book. The members of our Flickr group range from professional illustrators to folks who like to draw for fun. Remember, there's no 'right' or 'wrong' way to draw. A good drawing isn't necessarily a realistic or accurate one. Take a look at some artists' websites or a few blogs (and check out the drawings on the chapter opening pages of this book) and you'll see that there are about one million different illustration techniques*.

Use the template to sketch your day's outfit and fill in the blanks with your musings on that day in all its fashionista glory—the highs, the lows, and everything in between. Create your artwork using any media you can think of—paint, textiles, collage, or just plain old drawing—scan it in or photograph your drawing and upload to my site. Spend time browsing the blog—you might pick up some tips! Don't feel like sketching an entire outfit? Design your own pages to let you add individual items, from jewelry to a funky Halloween costume.

It's not only about the clothes—we've also included space for your favorite playlists, makeup looks, books, or style icons. Use the wishlists to scribble down handy notes, or glue in some great pictures from magazines or catalogs. Stick in fabric samples, note inspirational websites or sketch pattern designs…There are no dates— it's just helpfully arranged seasonally. Start in the middle, at the front, or near the back. There's space for a year's worth of fashion triumphs—and disasters. This journal is all about you, so be creative! Draw, cut 'n' stick, tear out pages if you want to, and use the book to have fun with fashion and drawing it too.

*Well, maybe not a MILLION, but there are loads!

MICHELLE LASALVIA (CHILE/CANADA)

JEN COLLINS (UK)

CRISTINA DE LERA (SPAIN)

BECKY GRAY (IRELAND)

LOGAN FAERBER (USA)

VICKY BARKER (UK)

Check out these spring styles for some inspiration –

THEN GET DRAWING!

YVONNE STEWART (UK)

DENISE HOLMES (USA)

SPRING

It's time to ditch the winter coat, scarf, and woolly hat... Spring is here at last! Spring is traditionally a time of new beginnings and new life (cue baby bunnies!), so use this season as an opportunity to reinvent your look. You could have a total makeover, try a new hairstyle (use our template to doodle your ideas!), or just add a bit more color to your wardrobe. Look around for inspiration: spring has sprung!

SWEATER
(it's a bit chilly today)

NEED A HAIRCUT

Umbrella
IN CASE OF
APRIL SHOWERS

HAND-PRINTED
Tote Bag

PUGS

Inspiration is everywhere—from pretty pink blossoms on the trees to bright, fun Easter eggs in the supermarket. So get outside in the fresh air, watch the new lambs frolic in the fields (city slickers: there's always You tube) and show off your finest springtime fashions. Take a look at the sample illustrations on page 10, check out the What I Wore Today group and blog, or flick through some magazines for inspiration.

bag for essential layers

Spring weather is predictably unpredictable. It can turn from sunny and warm to cloudy and cool pretty quickly, so always be prepared with a sweater or lightweight jacket in your bag. In case of April showers, don't forget your umbrella. One that neatly folds up to fit into your bag is useful if, like me, you're always leaving yours at work/school/the movies. We've created a template so that you can design your own.

Headgear comes into its own in spring: create your own designs and customize!

This is the traditional time of year to do some clearing out. Go through everything in your closet and give anything you don't wear to charity, or hold a clothing swap party with your friends.

ditchable items to free up closet space

Take a pile of clothes that you're tired of, or rarely wear, and swap them for something new (to you). After all, one girl's slightly-too-big orange halterneck minidress is another girl's show-stopper... or something like that.

Why not grab some fabric pens, sequins, and ribbons and spend a day customizing clothes and bags with your friends? You can buy a plain, eco-friendly, canvas tote bag from your local craft shop for less than the price of your weekly frappuccino.

Layers are everywhere: mix and match fabrics and colors

Sketch out your design using our template first, then get drawing/sticking/sewing... you'll be more than proud of your new, one-of-a-kind accessory. Another great activity to try with friends is jewelry making. Dig out your button collections, broken jewelry pieces and plastic cereal box charms. Since you're not hiding under layers of knitwear and a big old coat anymore (hopefully, but — like we said—who can count on the spring weather?), this is the perfect time to show off your beautiful, original handmade jewelry.

Spring is an optimistic and inspirational season, so enjoy yourself... Summer is on the way!

Sleeveless jackets and wintry boots: truly a wardrobe for all seasons

WHAT I WORE TODAY

Date: Location:

What are you doing? _____

_____

_____

Best Part of the Outfit

STYLE ICON OF THE DAY

Day into night—Jazz it up with a...

Necklace?   Boots?

14

...add your ideas here.

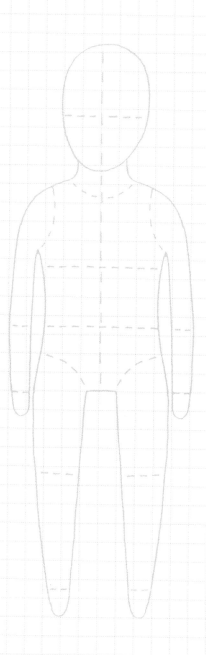

DESIGN YOUR OWN

TOTE BAG

Date: _____ Location: _____

Tote bags are an everyday essential—indispensable for carrying groceries, books, or small animals (maybe). They're the eco-friendly alternative to plastic bags, and sooo much more 'stylist', dahl-ing. Tote bags are usually made of a simple cotton canvas material, making them the perfect blank canvas (see what I did there?) for your most imaginative designs. They can be screen-printed, decorated with fabric pens, embellished with sequins, or appliquéd with textile scraps (a great way to use up any bits of pretty leftover fabric). Try a different design on each side so that you can flip it around according to your mood.

What's in your bag? _____

_____

_____

_____

DAY BAG

BEACH BAG

FESTIVAL BAG

TRY A TYPOGRAPHIC DESIGN HERE

WHAT I WORE TODAY

Date: _____ Location: _____

Outfit in a nutshell: _____

_____

_____

People-watching! Keep your eyes open today and doodle anyone you see whose style you like...

Add pets here!

Gemma's Hot Tips:

Sew or stick lace or ribbon to a jacket or pants for a superquick update. Accessorize with buttons, pins, and charms.

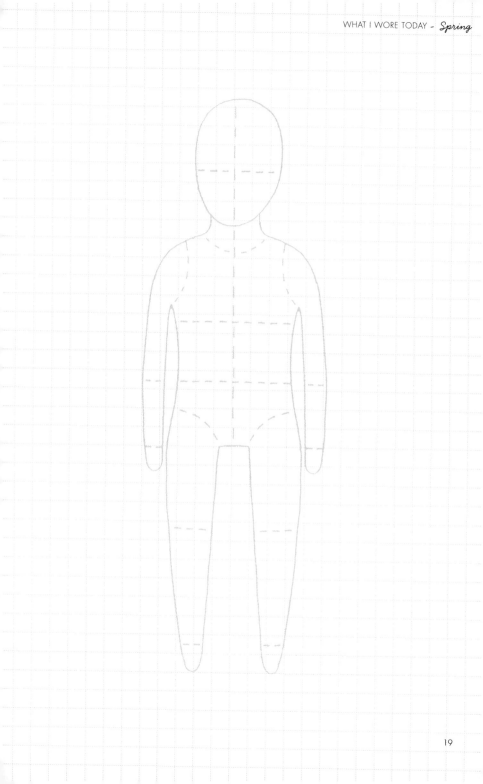

DESIGN YOUR OWN

UMBRELLA

Date: _____ Location: _____

Rainy days and April showers can be a lot of fun. Jumping in puddles, finding yourself unexpectedly taking shelter under a bus stop with a cute boy/girl, singing and dancing Gene Kelly-style... Not so enjoyable if you forget your umbrella, though, so keep a foldaway one stashed in your bag at all times. Using the template, try designing your own umbrella. You could design one that's traditionally multicolored, one with an allover pattern or animal print, or add some fabric flowers around the edge for a pretty, girly parasol that will make you smile, even when the sun has been in hiding for days. After you've perfected your design, why not sketch some matching boots to keep your feet dry in style, too?

Favorite lyric about the weather: _____

_____

_____

_____

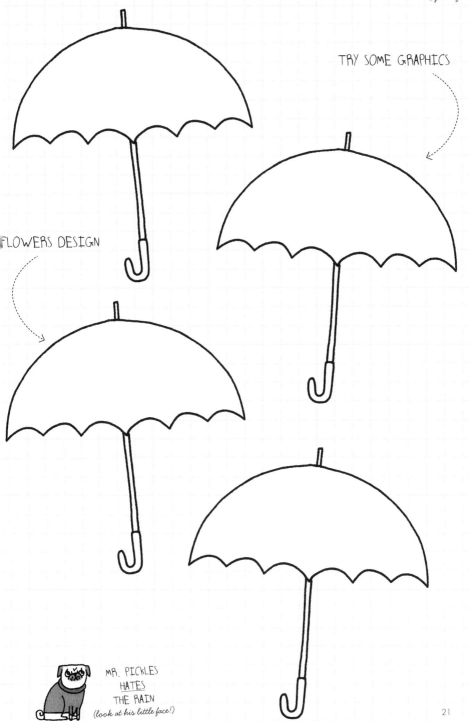

TRY SOME GRAPHICS

FLOWERS DESIGN

MR. PICKLES
<u>HATES</u>
THE RAIN
(look at his little face!)

21

WHAT I WORE TODAY

Date: _____ Location: _____ 👓

What are you doing? _____

_____

_____

PLAYLIST! Think about this one. 'Spring' is the theme but feel free to be abstract...

_____

_____

_____

_____

_____

_____

_____

Gemma's Hot Tips:

Natural fabrics are best (cheap and always stylish) when shopping for hats and other accessories. They mix and match well and can be dressed up or down.

Try dressing yourself as a rock star!

DESIGN YOUR OWN

HATS

Date: _____ Location: _____

A hat is another wardrobe essential for keeping off the chill or shading from those sunnier days. An outfit can be truly transformed by headgear. One with a wide brim will keep your face shaded from the sun and in the summer help keep your nose gloriously sunburn free. Try designing your own, by doodling an allover pattern or adding details like fun feathers or sparkly gemstones. Buy a simple hat (check thrift shops) and think about the fabric—should it be made of cotton, or maybe woven straw? Take inspiration from vibrant Mexican sombreros and decorate with metallic braid or colorful flowers, or keep it simple with a Panama-style straw hat. How about making your own rosettes or appliqué patches with pretty fabric scraps or bits of ribbon, and stick 'em on? Eco-friendly and beautiful. Hats off to you!

Hats are everywhere these days but can be tricky to pull off, style-wise. Who does it best and how?

_____

_____

_____

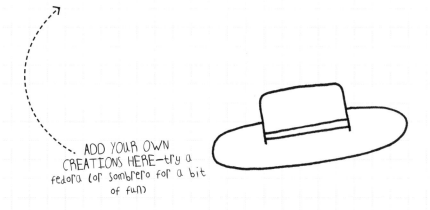

ADD YOUR OWN
CREATIONS HERE—try a
fedora (or sombrero for a bit
of fun)

WHAT I WORE TODAY

Date: _____   Location: _____

What are you doing? _____

_____

_____

WHAT MY BOYFRIEND/GIRLFRIEND/PET/MOM/BEST-FRIEND WORE
(delete as appropriate)

Now take a picture of your pet on your phone and send it on over!
(Check with his agent first, of course…)

FREESTYLE

||||||||||||||||||||||||||||||||||||||||||||||||||||||||||||||||||||||||||||||||||||||||||||||||||||||||

COSTUMES

Date: _____ Location: _____

Masquerade parties are fun during the Carnival season, but the variety
of potential costume ideas can be a bit overwhelming. It can be tricky
to narrow down a costume choice, especially if the party doesn't have
a theme. Take a look at some blogs for inspiration, or flip through your
movie/book/music collection for some costume ideas. Here are some of
our all-time favorite costumes: a Polaroid picture (supereasy to make with
a big piece of cardboard to frame your face); a Facebook page (again,
all you need is some cardboard and some pens: cut out a space for your
'profile picture' — i.e., your face—and go to town with the rest!); a candy
bar (of your choice!); and… well, any 1990s cartoon character. We're
sure you have some better ideas, though! Try designing your costume here
and you'll be the belle of the ball. Or at least, the girl, or boy-dressed-in-
some-kind-of-crazy-outfit of the ball.

So, what happened at the party? (There was a party, right?)

_____

_____

_____

WHAT I WORE TODAY

Date: _____ Location: _____

What are you doing? _____

_____

_____

Best Part of the Outfit

MAGAZINE

PUT YOURSELF ON THE COVER!

Spring Style Slogan—**SUM UP THE SEASON:**

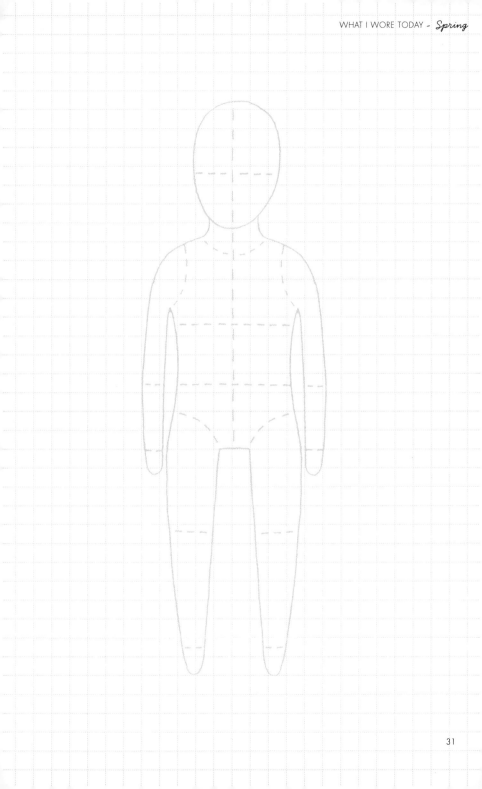

WISH LIST

Here's space to doodle those must-haves for next year.
Think about what to look out for in the sales, which
accessories you've coveted most, and the pieces that
you'd have on your imaginary (or real?) catwalk.

Highlights of the season (sartorial or otherwise):

_____

_____

_____

_____

_____

_____

SIMONE MASSONI (ITALY)

MICHELLE ALLBERRY (UK)

SHERRY YU (CHINA)

GINA LEE BEAN (UK)

MARLOES DE VRIES (THE NETHERLANDS)

JENNY McCLURE (UK)

Check out these summer styles for some inspiration...

THEN GET DRAWING!

SCARLETT TIERNEY (UK)

HANNAH READ (UK)

SUMMER

Whether you're spending your free time this summer frolicking on a beach, chilling out at a festival, or just relaxing at home, this season is all about easy, laid-back fashion, fun colors and keeping cool in every sense of the word.
Take a look at the WIWT blog for summer inspiration from all over the world. Look for contributions from the boys and girls who hail from sunny climates, like Australia or southern Europe, for tips on how to dress comfortably for hot weather.

SUNGLASSES
found at a
YARD SALE

necklace
(MADE WITH A SHELL FROM THE BEACH)

Dress
(MADE FROM AN OLD T-SHIRT)

FLIP-FLOPS

On those days when the thermometer is climbing, you'll probably want to stick to simple and minimal clothing—T-shirts, dresses, shorts—keeping your cool with lightweight, breathable, and natural fabrics like cotton and linen.

pet prints on T-shirts rock!

One of the easiest clothing items to customize is the summer staple: the humble T-shirt. You can dye it (even tie-dye it for that '70s hippie vibe), draw on it with fabric markers, appliqué onto it, or use iron-on transfers. Practice your design on the template in this section and make your own unique design.

Picnics are a fun excuse to wear a pretty summer dress and flowers in your hair. Keep a sweater or light jacket handy for cooler evenings.

If you're planning to spend time at the beach, of course you'll be needing suitable attire. Swimwear is essential, even if you don't intend to get anywhere near a giant inflatable crocodile (or, for that matter, a real one). Design your own bikini or swim shorts using the template in this section for a beach look that will impress from Hawaii to the Jersey shore. Always remember to take a cover-up with you (that's where your customized, oversized T-shirt might come in handy). Sunglasses are essential to help block out those harmful UV rays, which can damage your eyes. Buy a simple pair of plastic sunnies and cover them with sparkly gems for a summertime look that is sure to get you noticed. A big floppy sun hat, or a straw boater, is perfect for shading your face from the sun and is really easy to customize with fake flowers. Remember, the sun's rays are at their most dangerous between 12 and 3p.m., so keep yourself covered up and don't skimp on the sun cream.

For your poor neglected feet (it's been a while since they've seen the sunshine!), it's time to dig out the flip-flops. Customize yours using fake flowers or plastic gems. Or make like a Spanish señorita and don a pair of espadrilles. You could give your toenails a lick of pretty paint... There are tons of blogs dedicated to nail art, featuring some amazingly detailed designs, so get creative and have fun experimenting with colors and patterns... !

vintage shapes are must-haves

It's well known that light colors absorb less heat than darker ones, but be careful—if you're anything like me, the day you wear a white sundress will be the day you drop an entire strawberry and kiwi slushy down your front. Still, part of the fun of this book is documenting the mistakes, accidents, and general crumby stuff that happens to all of us. Artists draw upon bad experiences, such as having a bad hair day or standing in dog poop, for inspiration... It's called catharsis (and you're very welcome to use that in your next English essay). This isn't a glossy fashion mag—you're not going to end up in 'What was She Thinking?', so don't sweat the small stuff.

Grab an iced coffee and some sketching materials and go doodle outside in the sunshine... Don't forget the Factor 30!

WHAT I WORE TODAY

Date: _____ *Location:* _____

What are you doing? _____

_____

_____

HAIRCUTS: *They can be cuts you've seen or dos you've designed yourself. Make sure you give them each a name. There's room for three below, and you can try a new one on yourself opposite...*

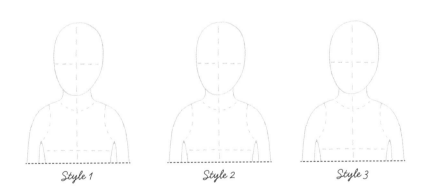

Style 1   *Style 2*   *Style 3*

Gemma's Hot Tips:

Collect buttons, ribbons and fabric scraps and store them in jars on your shelf for a pretty and practical display.

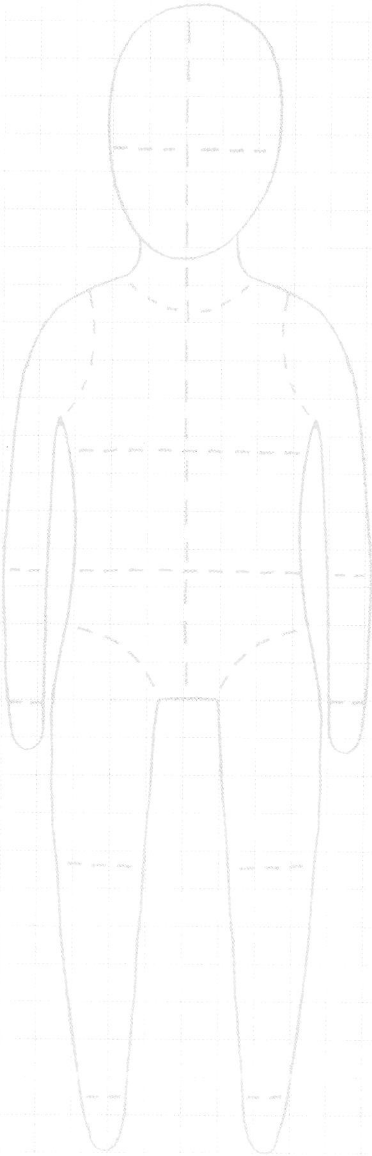

DESIGN YOUR OWN

T-SHIRTS

Date: __2/25/15__   Location: _____

T-shirts have to be the most versatile items of clothing out there. You can doodle on them with fabric pens, stencil onto them with spray paint, stick stuff on them, or cut them up and sew them back together again. You can dye them, tie-dye them, bleach them, or decorate them with '80s-style slogans … the list really is endless. Use the simple T-shirt template here to scribble your design and then move on to the real thing. You could print your design onto an inkjet transfer and then iron it onto your plain tee. If you don't feel like decorating your own, have a rummage around in some thrift shops for some cool old vintage tees. If the tees you find are too big, lop off the sleeves for a slouchy, oversized tank top, slash across the neck for an off-the-shoulder look, or cut out the design and use it as a patch for a bag or jacket. Have fun designing a top that will suit you to a T (shirt).

How do you wear yours? List your faves and what they go with:

_____

_____

_____

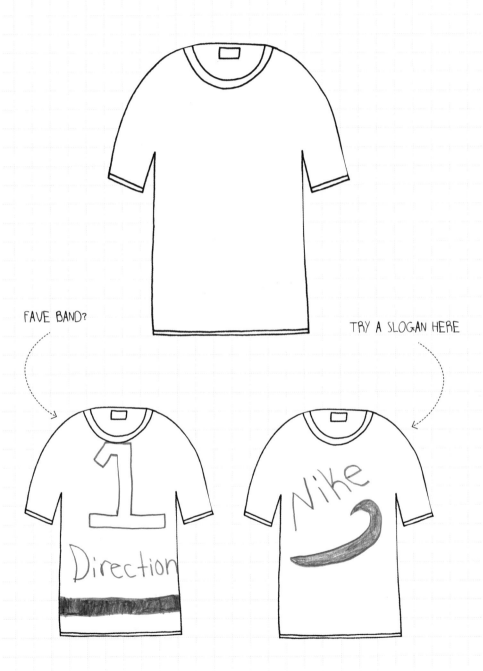

FAVE BAND?

TRY A SLOGAN HERE

WHAT I WORE TODAY

Date: _____ Location: _____

What are you doing? _____

_____

_____

PLAYLIST! Summer tunes! Try some classic '60s pop mixed with the latest sounds:

_____

_____

_____

_____

_____

_____

_____

_____

_____

_____

*Dress like a Vandella, a Beach Boy, or
anyone else who inspires you!*

DESIGN YOUR OWN

SWIMWEAR

Date: _____ Location:_____

Whether you're heading to the beach or just the local swimming pool, you'll probably be needing some swimwear... From polka-dot pinup girl-esque bikinis to cool surfer-style swim shorts, there's an enormous range of swimwear styles out there. Ignore boring magazine features on buying bikinis to 'suit your shape'—we think it's more important to have fun with your clothes, and that goes for swimwear too. Our advice is: if you like it, wear it! Design your own bikini or shorts using our template—try nautical stripes or graphic geometric shapes, or try mixing and matching colors and patterns for an eclectic look. Add quirky details with ribbon or beading, or collect some tiny seashells or pieces of sea glass from the beach and attach them around the edge of your bikini for a natural, laid-back look. Add some flip-flops and a sarong, grab an ice cream, and you're ready to go and soak up some sunshine!

Favorite beach snack: _____

_____

_____

_____ But watch out for seagulls!

You draw the bottoms...

Now come up with your own style...

TRY SOME DESIGNS FOR THE BOYS...

WHAT I WORE TODAY

Date: _____ *Location:* _____

What are you doing? _____

_____

_____

WHAT MY BOYFRIEND/GIRLFRIEND/PET/MOM/BEST FRIEND WORE

(delete as appropriate)

Now take a picture on your phone and send it on over!
(Share the love and try someone new this time.)

DESIGN YOUR OWN

SUNGLASSES

Who said 'Boys don't make passes at girls who wear glasses'? Whoever it was had obviously never met supercool four-eyes Chloe Sevigny or sexy spec-wearer Johnny Depp (yep, they definitely work for guys, too). The array of funky frames available at your friendly local optician/discount store/online retailer is enough to make even those blessed with 20/20 vision want to channel his/her inner Velma*. Glasses can really change the look of your face, depending on the size and shape of the frame. If you're a member of the 'lucky-me-I-have-perfect-vision' club, so no need for glasses, how about sketching some nifty sunglasses to block out those harmful UVB rays? Practice on our templates first, and then use a permanent marker to doodle your design onto some plain plastic frames, or glue on some crystals, buttons, or charms. *Snazzy!*

Date: _____   Location:_____

* That's Velma, the awesomely bespectacled lass from *Scooby Doo*, cartoon fans.

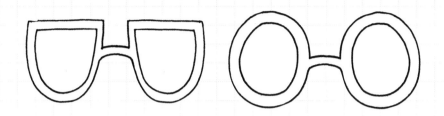

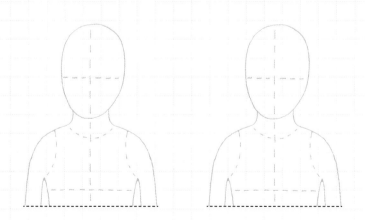

Now try some on…

49

WHAT I WORE TODAY

Date: _____ Location: _____

What are you doing? _____

_____

_____

Color is key! – MAKE YOUR OWN COLOR SWATCHES, THEN BASE YOUR OUTFIT AROUND THEM:

Try a strong first color, a complementary second color and some accents for accessories—or just clash, clash, clash!

Gemma's Hot Tips:

A soft vintage belt, a statement necklace, or glam bag, can turn a day-time outfit into an elegant evening look.

DESIGN YOUR OWN

WATCH

Date: 2/25/15 _____ Location: _____

Hey, what's the time? … Probably time you got a watch. Whether you're superpunctual or always the last to arrive, a wristwatch can be a functional and fashionable accessory. Watches can be analog or digital, with bands made of anything from shiny silver and beads to fun faux fur. Use the handy (ho ho!) template to design yourself a watch or two. You can also design some bracelets and bangles. Try doodling an old-school handmade friendship bracelet, a silver bangle adorned with kooky charms, or use shells, buttons, beads, and even candy—we've seen some amazing bracelets made from gummi bears! Yummy! Or get crafty with some papier-mâché and make a one-of-a-kind design that is entirely your own. You'll have the most gorgeous wrists in town.

If money was no object, my dream watch would be a...

_____

_____

_____

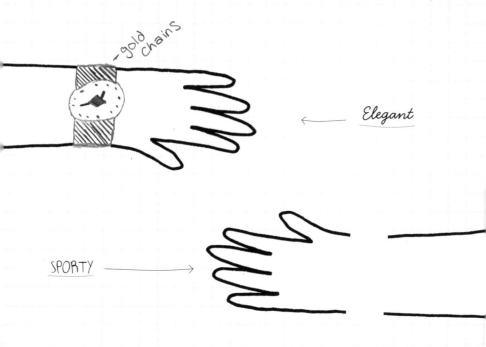

gold chains

Elegant ←

SPORTY →

TRY SOME **bigger** DESIGNS DOWN HERE...
↓ ↓ ↓ ↓ ↓ ↓ ↓ ↓ ↓ ↓ ↓ ↓

WHAT I WORE TODAY

Date: _____ Location: _____

What are you doing? _____

_____

_____

_____

What are your ultimate summer accessories?
LIST THEM *AND* DRAW THEM!

Mr Pickles
NEEDS NO MORE THAN A PAIR OF
SHADES AND HIS BIRTHDAY SUIT!

ADD YOURSELF INTO THE SCENE

FREESTYLE

||||||||||||||||||||||||||||||||||||||||||||||||||||||||||||||||||||||||||||||||||||||||||||||||||||||||

EVENING WEAR

Date: ——————————   *Location:* ———————————

It's party time! So you're going to need something to wear. Using
the basic dress template, try designing your dream party attire. Add
sequins for a festive, sparkly vibe, channel your inner Audrey Hepburn
with a classic Little Black Dress, or try a fabulous vintage fabric. What I
Wore Today-ers from the Flickr group have been known to make their own
frocks from old curtains, comforter covers, and even tablecloths. So check
out the linens section of your local thrift shop—just watch out for moth
holes! Look back to the 1980s and try a bubble skirt, or go for a
fabulously flirty '40s tea dress. Add some ace accessories, sweet shoes,
and jazzy jewelry and you'll be the belle of the ball... or the disco.

Come on, spill the beans. What happened last night?

————————————————————————————————

————————————————————————————————

————————————————————————————————

WISH LIST

Summer's all about dreaming up your own unique
fashion styles. Get inspiration from people-
watching and vintage shops, then mix-and-match:
take a casual '50s St Tropez look, add a touch
of '60s California cool, and change your hair
or outfit for the day... or even the whole season!

Highlights of the season (sartorial or otherwise):

_____

_____

_____

_____

_____

_____

LIZZY STEWART (UK)

DIOGO MACHADO (BRAZIL)

GIOVANA MILANESE (BRAZIL)

Check out these fall styles for some inspiration...

THEN GET DRAWING!

ALYSSA NASSNER (USA)

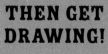

FALL

The days are getting shorter and there's a slight chill in the air... Fall has arrived. Hurrah! Watch the leaves change from green to brown... and red... and orange. This is a beautiful time of the year, so it's easy to feel inspired. There's no need to get rid of your summery clothes yet, just combine them with some warmer items for an easy between-seasons look. This season's weather, like spring's, can be a little unpredictable, so layers are the key.

Windproof Jacket (VERY IMPORTANT!)

Striped Top (FROM A CLOTHES SWAP)

BAG *accessorized with* BUTTONS

MR. PICKLES LOOKS WORRIED

(he doesn't like the rain)

Wear a windproof jacket over a sweater over a shirt over a... Well, you get the picture. Make it easy for yourself by being able to adjust your outfit to suit any weather or temperature. Wear tights under your shorts or layer a long-sleeved top under a short-sleeved T-shirt, etc., etc. It can get a bit breezy during fall, too, so make sure your jacket is windproof (and you may as well make sure it's waterproof too, while you're at it). Keep your toes dry while kicking leaves in the park by donning a pair of colorful rubber boots – you could even paint yours for some added fall fabulousness (try saying that ten times fast!).

headgear, undergarments and more accessories...hooray!!

Football games on chilly fall days just cry out for a cool knitted hat and a chunky scarf. Hey, you could even knit them yourself. If you've been invited to a Halloween party, you might want to design an outfit that will really make you stand out from all the zombies, witches, and random celebrity costumes. It can be tricky to narrow down a costume choice, especially if the party doesn't have a theme so always have a strong look in mind and follow it through!

Look through some magazines and blogs for inspiration, or flip through your movie/book/music collection for some ideas.

There's space for you to customize your jeans, design your own jewelry, create shirts, and hair-styles that willl see you through the difficult end-of-the-season where

Summer looks are out, but it's too warm for you to break out your Winter wardrobe.

Giant sweaters come into their own in fall, and it's a great time to pick up some cool outfits in the thrift shops. With people moving, and getting rid of old stuff, the end of summer is the best time to pick up great items to accessorize and inspire. Christmas doesn't seem so far away now, and people everywhere get inspired to put their best foot forward and get a completely new look for the season.

Wardrobe staples that haven't seen the light of day in all that sunny weather can be rediscovered, and thrift shops become treasure troves at this time of year (we can't think of a better way to escape the chill than rummaging in a vintage shop!).

Not going out very much? Snuggle up by the fire (or under the nearest blanket/comforter/large dog) with some hot chocolate and your preferred drawing medium and translate all those cozy thoughts into inspired autumnal outfit designs. In this section, we've included a template for you to design some funky underwear to lounge around the house in, plus some jeans and a shirt to complete your fall outfit. Go forth and doodle!

WHAT I WORE TODAY

Date: 11/11/14　　Location: Bedroom

What are you doing? _____

_____

_____

MAGAZINE - Now that you've graced the cover, here's your double-page spread. Try a couple of drawings and a list, or a little paragraph with a BIG first letter...

Gemma's Hot Tips:

Don't worry about hemming T-shirts—they don't fray and you'll end up with a cool rolled-hem look.

— Sweatshirt

— leggings

Try drawing a superglam high-fashion outfit.

DESIGN YOUR OWN

JEANS

Date: _____   Location: _____

Boot-cut, skinny, or low-rise, everyone has at least one pair of jeans in their wardrobe—they go with anything! Originally made for California miners in the 1850s, these days jeans are worn by folks of all ages from all over the world. Want yours to stand out from the crowd? Here are some ideas. Sketch a design onto jeans using tailor's chalk, and embroider over the top. Rub your jeans with sandpaper or a pumice stone to get a natural worn appearance. Attach pins, buttons, appliqué, and ribbon, or studs for a punky look. One easy way to update your jeans is simply to tie a scarf around the waist (take a look in your local thrift shops for cool vintage scarves at bargain prices)—no sewing required! And, if all else fails, chop the legs off and make some cool cutoff shorts. Use the template to design your perfect pair of denims and then try customizing yours for real.

Do the perfect jeans exist? What is your fave style?

_____

_____

_____

*These are kind of classic jeans,
but how about a bright color?*

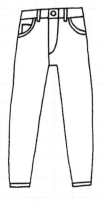

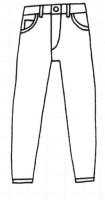

*Try drawing yourself
into this pair.*

Add some new cuts to these— try flares, drainpipes, whatever you like!

WHAT I WORE TODAY

Date: _____ Location: _____

What are you doing? _____

_____

_____

Best Part of the Outfit

STYLE ICON OF THE DAY

Mr. Pickles

HAS A RANGE OF CHUNKY AUTUMNAL
KNITS FOR WHEN HE GETS CHILLY.

Do you have a pet that would look good in a sweater?

FREESTYLE

JEWELRY

Date: ——————————— *Location:*———————————

Diamonds may be a girl's best friend (we're pretty sure that it's ice cream, though), but we think plastic charms, wooden beads, and vintage cameos are just as interesting. Buy from craft fairs, flea markets and antique fairs, or from online craft shops such as Etsy for one of-a-kind, handmade pieces. Or, make your own! You can make jewelry from just about anything— from paper clips (clip them together to make a necklace or bracelet) to plastic bags (cut them into strips and braid them together). You can hand- draw designs onto shrink plastic and then punch holes to make unique pendants and pins, or mold beads and charms from polymer clay. Keep a stash of buttons, sequins, charms, lace, and ribbon scraps handy for creative days, and recycle broken jewelry by taking it apart and using it to make new stuff.

Jewelry this good requires the perfect occasion. Mine would be...

———————————————————————————

———————————————————————————

———————————————————————————

WHAT I WORE TODAY

Date: _____ Location: _____

What are you doing? _____

_____

_____

People-watching! Slight twist this time: eyes peeled for a cool-looking couple to doodle...

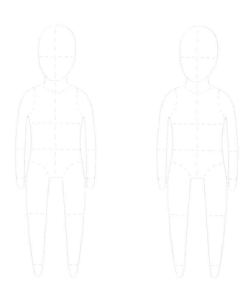

Gemma's Hot Tips:

Find new ways to use accessories — try using a scarf as a belt, or a necklace as a hairband.

DESIGN YOUR OWN

SHIRTS

Date: _____ *Location:* _____

Checked, denim, white, or colored, the shirt is a wardrobe staple and can be dressed up or down. Tie a ribbon around the neck for a French-inspired look, or appliqué with shaped fabric patches. Try replacing the shirt's buttons with different ones. You can find interesting and unusual buttons in thrift stores and craft stores, or you can make your own using polymer clay. Just make sure they fit in the buttonholes! Think about what fabric your ideal shirt might be made of, and when and where you might wear it, then design it using the template.

Your top ten shirt-wearers? _____

_____

_____

_____

FORMAL COLORS

With a tie, perhaps?

Or maybe short-sleeved?

Fun patterns!

WHAT I WORE TODAY

Date: _____ Location: _____

What are you doing? _____

_____

_____

PLAYLIST! Don't worry if you can't think of anything now. You have the whole season to fill this in…

_____

_____

_____

_____

_____

_____

_____

_____

_____

_____

_____

DESIGN YOUR OWN

HAIRSTYLES

Date: _____ Location:_____

Are you bored with your bob? Dissatisfied with your dreadlocks? With
our template, your can doodle yourself into hairdo heaven. Wield some
imaginary scissors and give yourself bangs or a sweet '60s-style updo,
or channel your inner rock star and draw something totally wild with crazy
colors and outrageous accessories. If you've always yearned for a pixie
crop, or blue highlights, here's your chance to try them out without setting
foot in the hair salon. Think about what products you might need to use
to create your hairstyle, then write them down, or draw them. Hairspray?
Curling tongs? Maybe some henna? If you're not feeling that adventurous,
keep the hair simple and try designing some beautiful barrettes,
a fabulously retro fascinator, or a nifty head scarf. Now you'll never
have a bad hair day again!

My worst haircut ever was... _____

_____

_____

_____ *Find a pic and stick it in!*

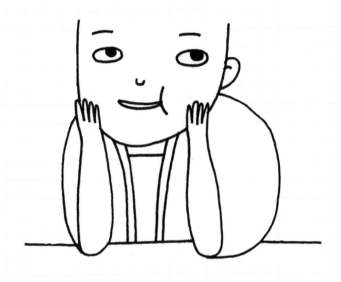

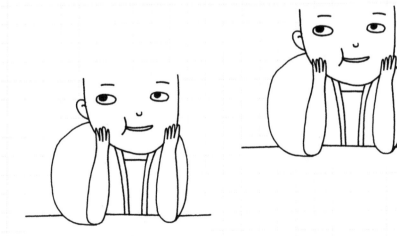

WHAT I WORE TODAY

Date: _____ Location: _____

What are you doing? _____

_____

_____

_____

What are your ultimate fall accessories?

LIST THEM *AND* DRAW THEM!

Gemma's Hot Tips:

Classic styles are best for hats, and other accessories. Think about your favorite outfits and how they will match before taking the leap.

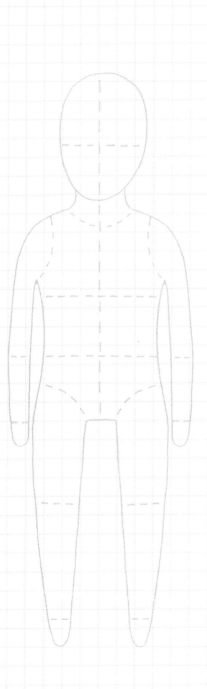

FREESTYLE

||||||||||||||||||||||||||||||||||||||||||||||||||||||||||||||||||||||||||||||||||||||||||||||||||||||||||||||||||||||

UNDERWEAR

Date: _____ *Location:* _____

Bras, panties and tank tops, oh my! Underwear, or *lingerie* if we're being fancy, is the one thing that we all wear, all year round. With the minimum of fabric, clever designer types have created quirky, innovative styles, from funky cartoon-emblazoned panties made from old T-shirts to beautiful handcrafted 1940s-style brassieres and corsets. Have fun designing your own—as long as you're comfortable, anything goes. Try different colors and patterns, add some lace, embroidery, or iron-on transfers and you'll have some undies that you won't want to keep hidden under your clothes. Whether or not you're an underwear as outerwear kinda person, underwear should make you want to hang them on your clothesline. While your neighbors blush, you'll be glowing with pride!

Embarrassing underwear story? Come on, everyone has one…

_____

_____

_____

WISH LIST

· ·

OK. Time to get inspired and dream up your own
Fall Collection. Forget the mayhem that grips the fashion
world at this time of year. You can take your time and
doodle until the cows come home... Mooo!

Random Quotes and Notes _____

_____

_____

_____

NEIL SLORANCE (UK)

JO WANT (UK)

JESSICA POTTS (USA)

NANNA KOEKOEK (UK/THE NETHERLANDS)

ANKE WECKMANN (UK)

MAIR THOMAS (UK)

Check out these winter styles for some inspiration...

THEN GET DRAWING!

CAROLINE WELLER (UK)

NIINA AOKI (AUSTRALIA)

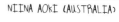

WINTER

It's winter and it's f-f-f-freezing! Whether you're braving the cold to build a snowman, going ice skating with friends, or walking to the supermarket, keeping warm is essential. You get to wear the maximum number of clothing items during winter, so make the most of it. Bundle up in sweaters, thick tights, and comfy boots, cover up with a warm coat (try designing your own with one of our templates) and wrap a chunky hand-knitted scarf or cowl around your neck.

SLIGHTLY *grumpy face*

HAT *knitted by my* BEST FRIEND

EXTRA-WARM COAT

Coffee (ESSENTIAL)

(ON MR PICKLES) *Sweater* PUGS GET _cold_ TOO!

D on't forget—60% of your body heat escapes through your head, so a nice cozy hat is a must, too. Try embellishing a plain beret with some colored sequins, for a fun accessory with a bit of added ooh-la-la. Or knit your own funky pom-pom hat with some colorful yarn wool and make use of those pom-pom-making skills you acquired at elementary school. Add some gloves or mittens and you'll be as toasty as a… umm, toast.

One of the loveliest things about winter is snuggling up under a cozy blanket with your favorite magazine and a warm drink (make ours a hot chocolate with extra marsh-mallows, please!) Make the most of it with comfy PJs and supersoft fluffy slippers or socks. If you're outdoors, be careful when negotiating icy pavements—make sure your shoes have some good grip to avoid taking an embarrassing tumble. Or simply score soles with a knife (be careful though).

Christmas is not all about sweaters: try knitting a scarf and glove set, and if you make a hat, remember the pom-pom!

There's no way to avoid it, Christmas is coming… which means munching on gingerbread (yum!), singing carols around a tree (maybe), and wearing funky festive fash-ions. This is the one time of year when wearing tinsel in your hair and flashing Santa Claus earrings is accept-able… although, hey, who are we to judge? If you feel like rocking those glittery reindeer socks during August, go for it! Another seasonal favorite is the Christmas

cardies, coats and fancy footwear

sweater, beloved of grannies and distant relatives everywhere. But, hey, if you can't beat 'em, join 'em, and we've included a page to design your very own.

Christmas also means giving gifts, which means shopping, but it can be just as much fun and cheaper (and less stressful than braving the frenzied festive shopping crowds) to make gifts for your friends and family. You could even use the templates and useful tips in this book as inspiration. Design a cool T-shirt for your best friend, brother, or dog (yep, they make T-shirts for our furry friends too, dontcha know) using our handy template and then grab some fabric pens to doodle your design for real. Or try your hand at some embroidery and make a pretty tank top, change purse or scarf. You could make it your mission to use recycled materials only—plastic bags woven together make great bracelets, and fabric scraps are perfect for making sweet pins. Folks really like handmade gifts, and you'll have fun making them, too.

coats are the ultimate fashion staple. The bigger the better!

The What I Wore Today Flickr group and blog are full of ideas for dressing for the chilly season, so if you're feeling a bit stuck, head on over there for some inspiration. What are you waiting for? Grab your art materials and curl up somewhere warm and comfy to sketch, scribble, and create the hours away.

WHAT I WORE TODAY

Date: _____ Location: _____

What are you doing? _____

_____

_____

PLAYLIST! When it is cold outside, think of some songs to make you feel warm inside:

_____

_____

_____

_____

_____

_____

_____

_____

_____

_____

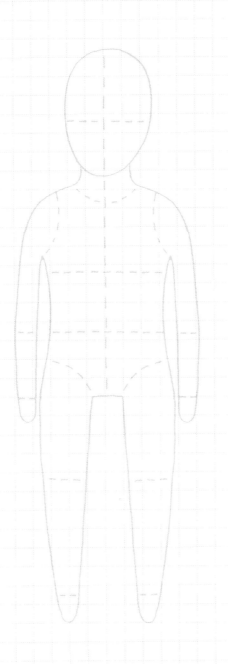

Dress for maximum warmth: go for a HUGE scarf!

DESIGN YOUR OWN

SCARF/HAT/GLOVES

Date: _____ Location:_____

One of the best things about winter is getting to dress up in lovely, cozy
knitted things like hats, scarves, and gloves. If you know how to knit or
crochet, you could make your winter accessories yourself. Look
at existing knitwear designs for inspiration—from Fair Isle knits to argyle
patterns. Pom-poms are fun and easy to make—try making one with multicolored or glittery yarn and attach it to your hat. Use this template
to doodle your perfect winter warmers.

When it is cold outside, the coziest place to be is...

_____

_____

_____

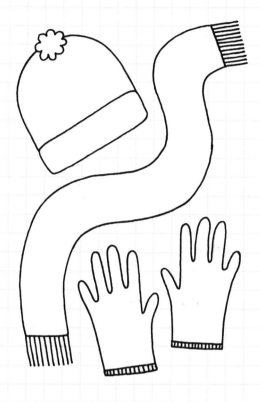

Mr. Pickles
ALWAYS LOOKS DISTINGUISHED
IN THE WINTER MONTHS

WHAT I WORE TODAY

Date: _____ Location: _____

What are you doing? _____

_____

_____

Duffle, trench, swing, or parka... a good coat will keep you warm, dry, and
happy, so start doodling, or stick in some pics from magazines:

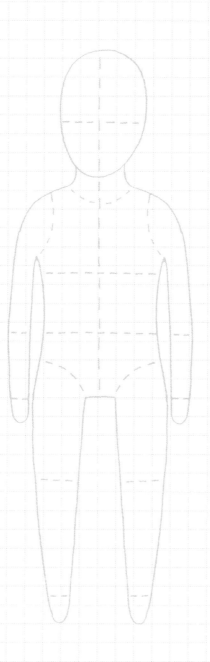

DESIGN YOUR OWN

~~~~~~

POCKETS

Date: _____ Location:_____

Pockets are a useful addition to any clothing item (with the possible
exception of socks…). Doodle around these predrawn pockets and
create a clothing item of your choice—from a jacket to a jumper
dress. You could draw the stuff that you keep in your pockets, too,
like pens or keys or hamsters …

Pocket essentials—list what you keep in yours…

_____

_____

_____

Try one top and some bottoms, or one boys' thing and one girls'…

WHAT I WORE TODAY

Date: _____ Location: _____

What are you doing? _____

_____

_____

WHAT I SHOULD NOT HAVE WORN! *Draw one of your mistakes...*

...and remember that mistakes happen. You should never be afraid to experiment... Just don't wear this one again!

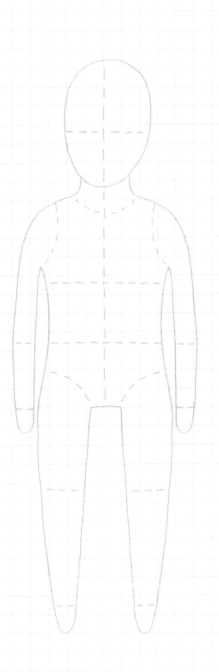

DESIGN YOUR OWN

CHRISTMAS SWEATER

Date: _____ Location: _____

Ahh, Christmas… It's a time for singing carols, celebrating with friends and family, and eating too much turkey and drinking too much eggnog. Practice your look of joy when that distant aunt of yours inevitably gives you yet another size-too-small hand-knitted Christmas sweater featuring some sort of deformed reindeer pattern (or are those things supposed to be cats?).

So, here's your chance—design your very own festive sweater. Maybe you could even tactfully show your design to Aunt Harriet, so that next year you stand a chance of receiving something that you'd actually be proud to wear for the festive season, and beyond… or at least until New Year. And remember, at Christmas, anything goes—so go crazy with sequins, glitter, and crazy colors—but maybe go easy on the deformed reindeer.

The best thing about Christmas is…

_____

_____

_____

I WANTED THIS...

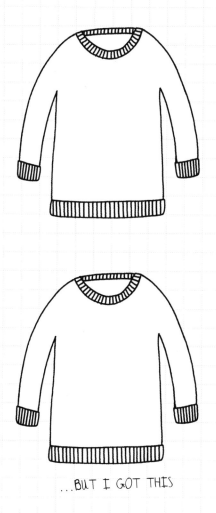

...BUT I GOT THIS

WHAT I WORE TODAY

Date: _____ Location: _____

What are you doing? _____

_____

_____

Color is key! OK, SO THIS TIME WORK UP SOME WINTER SHADES, BUT TRY A SPLASH OF SOMETHING BRIGHT & BOLD.

Try to use colors that feature on the clothes you have, or even clothes you want. Once you get the hang of matching colors, you will start to see possibilities everywhere!

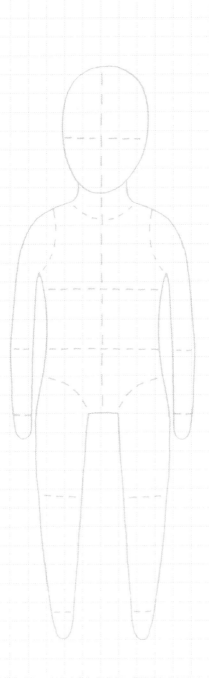

DESIGN YOUR OWN

~~~~~~~~~~~~~~~~~~~~~~~~~~~

SOCKS

Date: _____ Location: _____

Ankle, knee length, or thigh-high, socks keep your feet warm and dry, which is important during the cold winter months. With the hundreds of cute sock designs available, you can declare your love of everything from multicolored frogs to retro robots via your tootsies. Try designing your own, with an allover repeat pattern, zany zigzags, or good old-fashioned stripes. You could even embroider your socks with sequins and colored thread, or attach mini pom-poms or some lace, for delightful designs that will really... knock your socks off.

Your most rockin' socks ... _____

_____

_____

_____

Try drawing some with shoes...

Try drawing lacy ones for a night out...

WHAT I WORE TODAY

Date: _____ Location: _____

What are you doing? _____

_____

_____

WINTER REQUIRES *A LOT* OF PREPARATION. *What's in your bag today?*

LIST: DRAWINGS:

_____

_____

_____

_____

_____

_____

Gemma's Hot Tips:

If you're always losing your gloves, sew your knits to a length of cord or wool, attaching a glove to each end. Thread the mits down the arms of your coat and round the back so you don't drop them in a puddle!

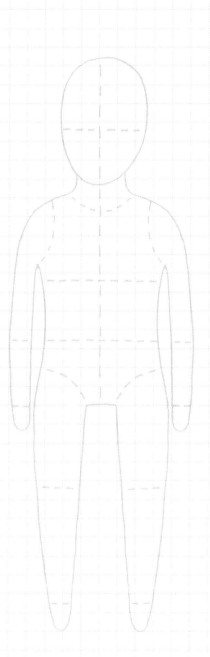

FREESTYLE

||||||||||||||||||||||||||||||||||||||||||||||||||||||||||||||||||||||||||||||||||||||||||||||||||||||

BUTTONS

Date: _____ Location:_____

Buttons are great! Especially when you need to accessorize in a hurry!
Regular sew-on buttons can do so much more than just keep your clothes
together! They can be sewn onto shirts or sweaters, threaded onto wire or
ribbon to make distinctive jewelry pieces. Doodle yourself into the scene
and you'll be looking as cute as a button.

Random Quotes and Notes _____

_____

_____

_____

WISH LIST

Here's some space to doodle those must-haves for next year. Think about what to look for in the sales, which accessories you've coveted most, and the pieces that you'd have on your imaginary (or real?) catwalk.

Random Quotes and Notes _____

_____

_____

_____

ACKNOWLEDGMENTS

Thank you to Eoghan and Sarah at Octopus Publishing for all your help in making this book a reality.

Thanks to everybody who has contributed their drawings to the What I Wore Today Flickr group and especially to Kuky for your assistance in moderating the group.

Thanks to the folks at the Little Red Roaster, Norwich, for keeping me caffeinated and entertaining me every day with your beautiful singing and skillful dance routines.

And of course, thank you to both Anthony and Mr Pickles, for keeping me company in the studio (and in life in general) and for cheering me up when I'm fed up and/or suffering from chocolate withdrawal symptoms.

Bye everyone, hopefully we will see you soon!

Gemma Correll (and Mr Pickles)